$15.95

What's Inside Me?
My Skin

¿Qué hay dentro de mí?
La piel

Dana Meachen Rau

Marshall Cavendish
Benchmark
New York

My Skin

La piel

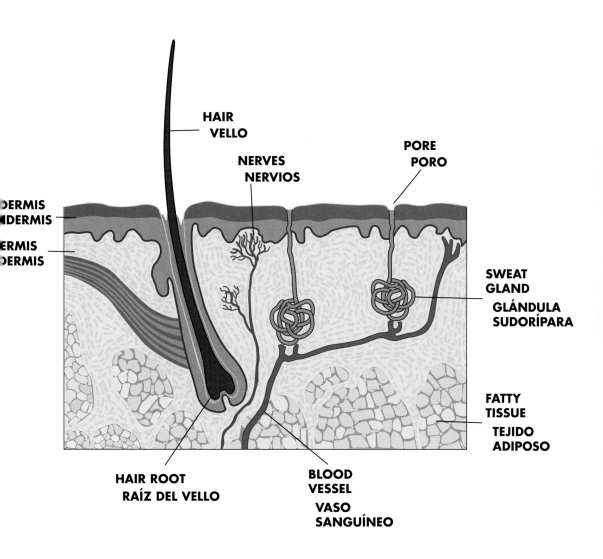

HAIR
VELLO

NERVES
NERVIOS

PORE
PORO

DERMIS
DERMIS

ERMIS
DERMIS

SWEAT
GLAND
GLÁNDULA
SUDORÍPARA

FATTY
TISSUE
TEJIDO
ADIPOSO

HAIR ROOT
RAÍZ DEL VELLO

BLOOD
VESSEL
VASO
SANGUÍNEO

3

There is a lot going on inside your body. Your body is filled with blood, bones, and *organs*.

All your organs have important jobs to do. Your lungs help you breathe. Your heart pumps your blood.

Muchas cosas pasan dentro del cuerpo. Tu cuerpo está lleno de sangre, huesos y *órganos*.

Todos los órganos hacen trabajos importantes. Los pulmones te ayudan a respirar. El corazón bombea tu sangre.

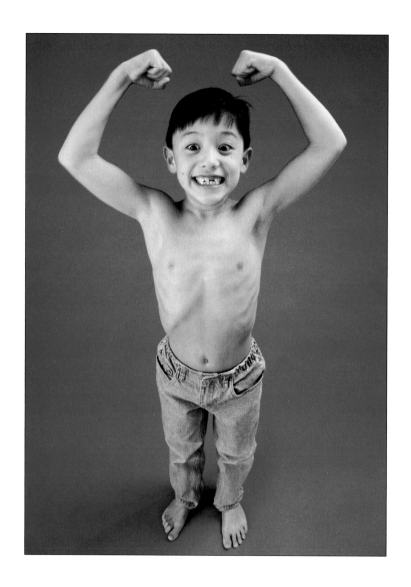

Your skin is your largest organ. It covers your whole body. It is in charge of protecting all your inside parts.

La piel es el órgano más grande de todos. Cubre todo el cuerpo para proteger todas las partes internas.

Germs are all around us. Germs can make you sick. Your skin keeps germs out of your body.

---❖---

Los *gérmenes* están a nuestro alrededor. Ellos te pueden enfermar. La piel mantiene a los gérmenes fuera de tu cuerpo.

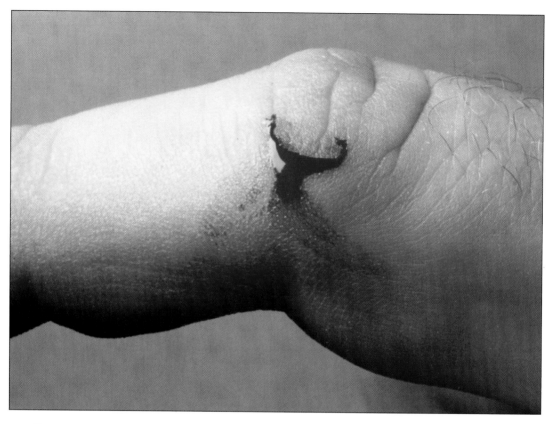

Germs can get into a cut in your skin.

Los gérmenes pueden entrar por las heridas de la piel.

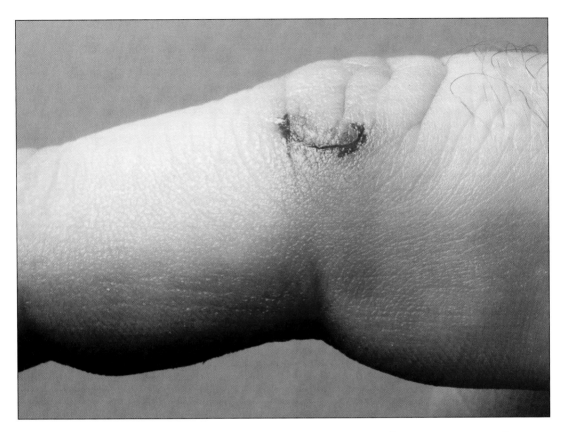

Blood forms a scab to plug up the cut and keep the germs out.

❖

La sangre forma una costra que tapa la herida y deja a los gérmenes fuera.

The skin you see on the outside of your body is called your epidermis. Your *epidermis* is made up of tiny *cells*.

The cells of your epidermis are dead. Millions of these dry dead cells fall off your body every day.

❖

La parte de la piel que puedes ver sobre tu cuerpo se llama *epidermis*. La epidermis está formada por pequeñas *células*.

En la epidermis hay células muertas. Todos los días, millones de células secas y muertas caen del cuerpo.

There is another layer of skin under the epidermis. This living inside layer is called the *dermis*. It makes millions of new skin cells every day.

The dermis is filled with little tubes that carry blood. These tubes are called *blood vessels*.

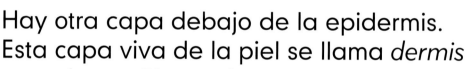

Hay otra capa debajo de la epidermis. Esta capa viva de la piel se llama *dermis* y produce millones de nuevas células todos los días.

La dermis está llena de pequeños tubos que transportan sangre. Estos tubos se llaman *vasos sanguíneos*.

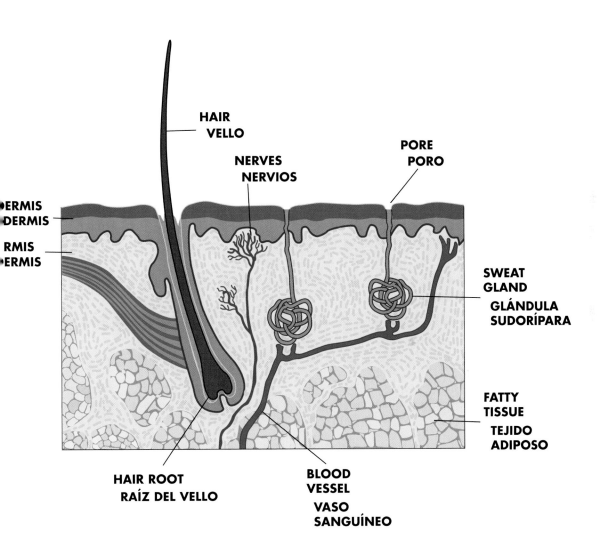

HAIR
VELLO

NERVES
NERVIOS

PORE
PORO

●ERMIS
●DERMIS

RMIS
●ERMIS

SWEAT
GLAND

GLÁNDULA
SUDORÍPARA

FATTY
TISSUE

TEJIDO
ADIPOSO

HAIR ROOT
RAÍZ DEL VELLO

BLOOD
VESSEL

VASO
SANGUÍNEO

15

Your dermis also has *nerves*. Nerves help you feel if something is rough or smooth.

La dermis también tiene *nervios*. Los nervios te ayudan a sentir si algo es áspero o suave.

They help you feel if something is hot
or cold.

❖

Te ayudan a sentir si algo está frío
o caliente.

Your skin is covered with tiny hairs. Only the palms of your hands and the bottoms of your feet do not have hair.

The roots of the hair are deep in the dermis. The roots are alive. But the hair outside the skin is dead.

La piel está cubierta de pelitos llamados vellos. Sólo las palmas de las manos y las plantas de los pies no tienen vellos.

Las raíces de los vellos están en lo profundo de la dermis. Ellas están vivas, pero el vello fuera de la piel está muerto.

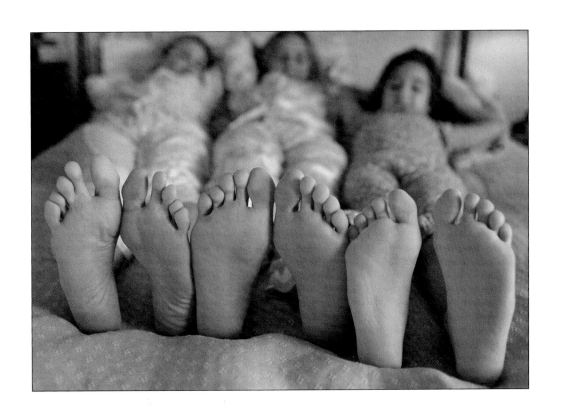

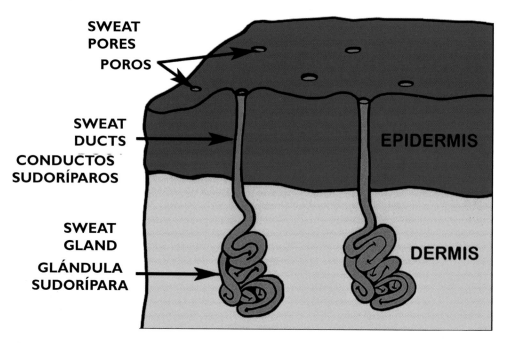

SWEAT PORES
POROS

SWEAT DUCTS
CONDUCTOS SUDORÍPAROS

SWEAT GLAND
GLÁNDULA SUDORÍPARA

EPIDERMIS

DERMIS

Your skin is filled with *sweat glands*. Sweat comes out of the sweat glands through a hole in your skin. This hole is called a *pore*.

❖

La piel está llena de *glándulas sudoríparas*. El sudor sale de las glándulas sudoríparas a través agujeritos en la piel llamados *poros*.

20

Sweating keeps your body cool when you get hot.

❖

Sudar mantiene el cuerpo fresco cuando hace calor.

All people have different colored skin. *Melanin* gives skin its color.

People with dark skin have a lot of melanin. People with light skin have just a little.

Freckles are spots with a lot of melanin.

Todas las personas tienen distintos colores de piel. La *melanina* le da el color a la piel.

Las personas de piel oscura tienen mucha melanina. Las personas de piel clara tiene sólo un poco.

Las pecas son puntos con mucha melanina.

The sun makes your skin create more melanin. If you have light skin and sit outside in the sun, your skin might get darker. This is called tanning.

El sol hace que la piel produzca más melanina. Si tu piel es clara y te sientas al sol, tu piel puede oscurecerse. Esto se llama bronceado.

But the sun can hurt your skin, too. Sunburn makes your skin turn red.

The top layer of your skin may peel, and your skin will sting.

Pero el sol también puede lastimar la piel. El sol puede quemarla y enrojecerla.

La capa externa de la piel puede pelarse y causar ardor.

Your skin protects you. It is important for you to protect your skin, too.

La piel te protege. Es importante que tú también protejas tu piel.

Challenge Words

blood vessels Little tubes that carry blood.

cells The tiniest building blocks of life that make up all living things.

dermis The living inside layer of skin.

epidermis The dead outer layer of skin.

germs Something that can make you sick.

melanin The material that gives skin color.

nerves Wire-like cords that run to all parts of your body.

organs Parts of your body with special jobs.

pore A tiny hole in your skin that lets out sweat.

sweat glands Tubes deep in the dermis that make sweat.

Palabras avanzadas

células Las diminutas partículas de vida que forman a todos los seres vivos.

dermis La capa interna y viva de la piel.

epidermis La capa externa y muerta de la piel.

gérmenes Los organismos que pueden provocar enfermedades.

glándulas sudoríparas Los tubos profundos de la piel que producen sudor.

melanina La sustancia del cuerpo que le da color a la piel.

nervios Los cordones parecidos a cables que llegan a todas las partes del cuerpo.

órganos Las partes del cuerpo que realizan un trabajo específico.

poros Los agujeritos de la piel por los que sale el sudor.

vasos sanguíneos Los pequeños tubos que transportan sangre.

Index

Índice

With thanks to Nanci Vargus, Ed.D. and Beth Walker Gambro, reading consultants

Marshall Cavendish Benchmark
99 White Plains Road
Tarrytown, New York 10591-9001
www.marshallcavendish.us

Library of Congress Cataloging-in-Publication Data

Rau, Dana Meachen, 1971–
[My skin. Spanish & English]
My skin = La piel / Dana Meachen Rau. — Bilingual ed.
p. cm. — (Bookworms. What's inside me? = ¿Qué hay dentro de mí?)
Includes index.
ISBN-13: 978-0-7614-2484-0 (bilingual edition)
ISBN-10: 0-7614-2484-9 (bilingual edition)
ISBN-13: 978-0-7614-2406-2 (Spanish edition)
ISBN-10: 0-7614-1778-8 (English edition)
1. Skin—Juvenile literature. I. Title. II. Title: La piel. III. Series:
Rau, Dana Meachen, 1971– Bookworms. What's inside me? (Spanish & English)

QP88.5.R3818 2006b
612.7'9—dc22
2006016714

Spanish Translation and Text Composition by Victory Productions, Inc.
www.victoryprd.com

Photo Research by Anne Burns Images

Cover Photo by *Corbis*/Royalty Free

The photographs in this book are used with the permission and through the courtesy of:
Corbis: pp. 1, 23 Laura Doss; p. 2 Anthony Nex; pp. 5, 9 Royalty Free; p. 6 Luis Pelaez; p. 12 Rob & Sas; p. 16 Tom Stewart; p. 17 Ed Bock; p. 19 L. Clarke; p. 21 Tim Pannell; p. 24 Wartenberg/Picture Press; p. 27 Bohemian Nomad Picturemakers; p. 28 Ariel Skelley. *Photo Researchers*: pp. 10, 11 Eric Schrempp. *Custom Medical Stock Photo*: p. 20.

Series design by Becky Terhune
Illustrations by Ian Warpole

Printed in Malaysia
1 3 5 6 4 2